One Tortoise, Ten Wallabies

A Wildlife Counting Book

by Jakki Wood

Bradbury Press
New York

1 one slow tortoise   **2** two hopping hares

3 three flying ducks   **4** four frisky, frolicsome foxes

5 five rollicking, rascally raccoons

6 six swinging, clinging, mischievous monkeys

7 seven squawking, talking toucans

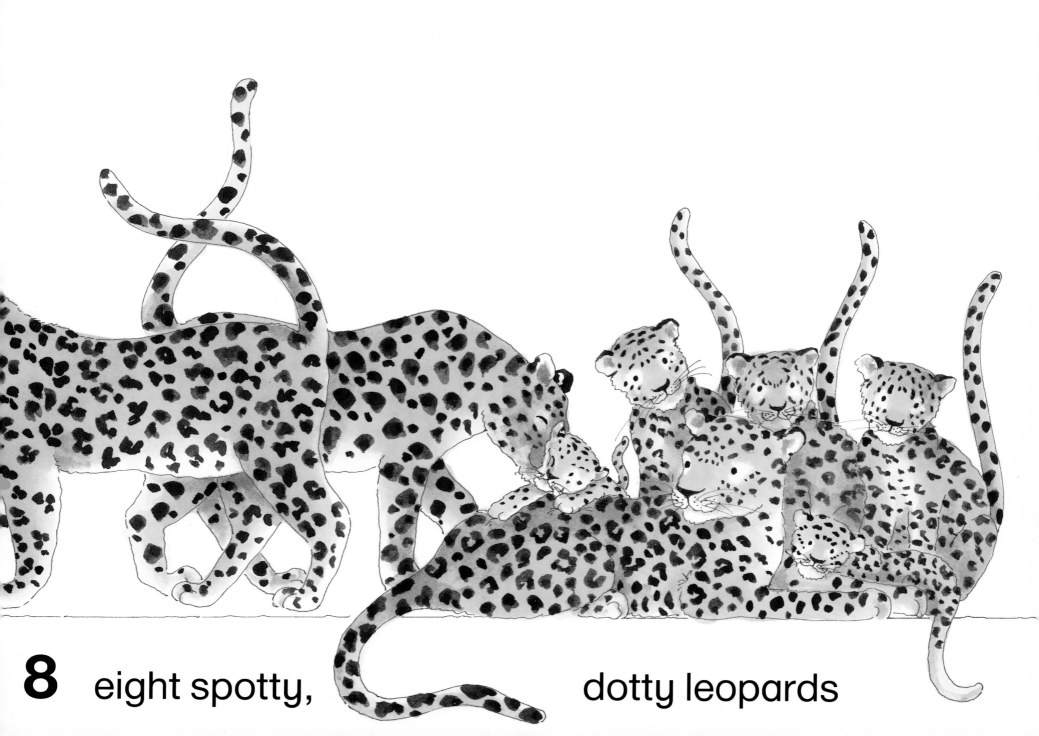

8 eight spotty,   dotty leopards

9 nine flip-flappy, slip-slappy seals

10 ten bouncing, bopping wallabies

11 eleven splish-splashing,

dip-diving   dolphins

12 twelve   neck-stretchy,   long-leggy,

pecky, **feathery** **ostriches**

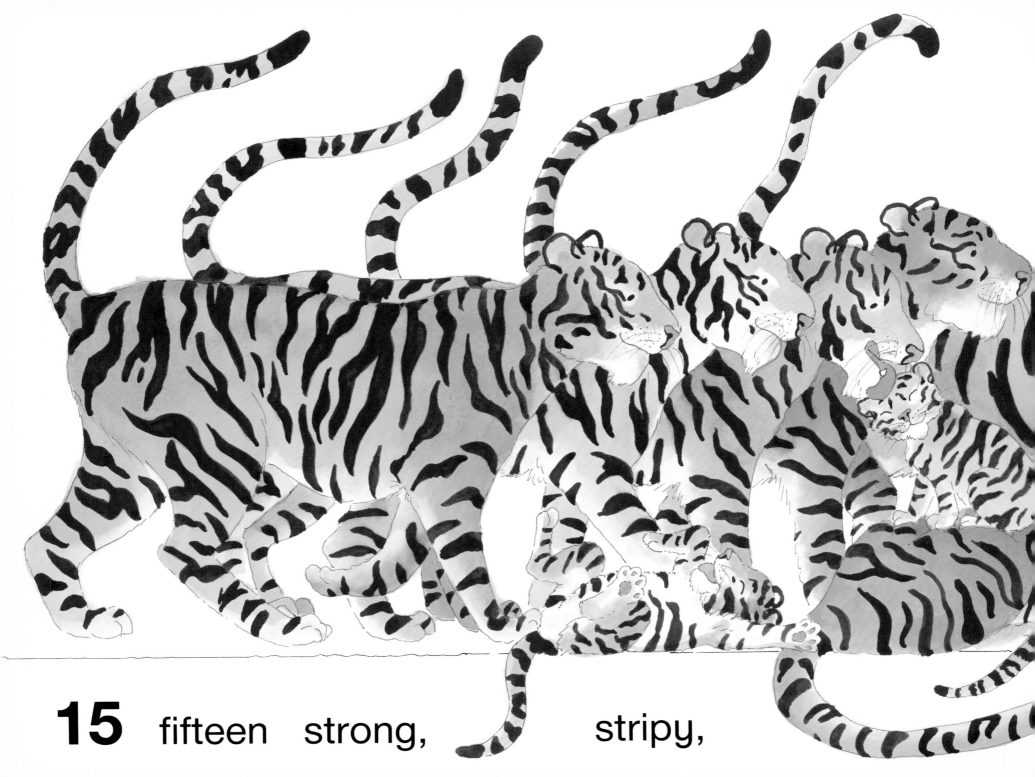

15 fifteen strong, stripy,

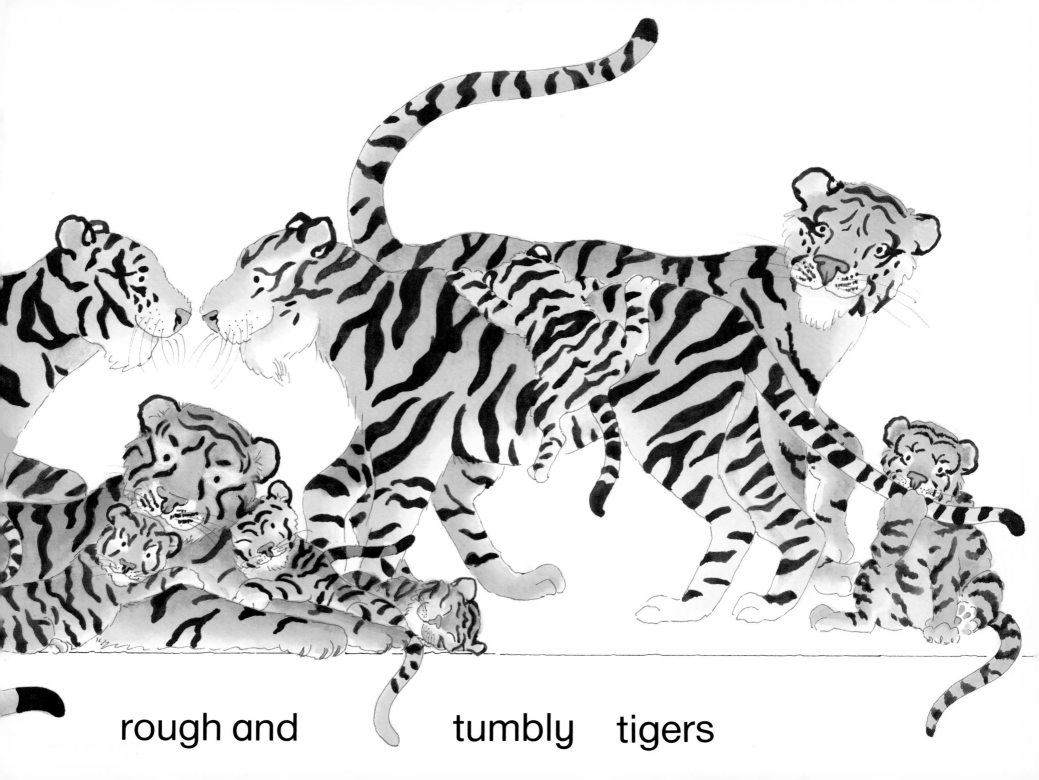

rough and tumbly tigers

20 twenty   hairy,   scary,   grinning,

growly   bears

25 twenty-five   humpy,   bumpy,

lanky, cranky camels

50 fifty   lumpy,   lazy,   hefty,

hearty   hippopotamuses

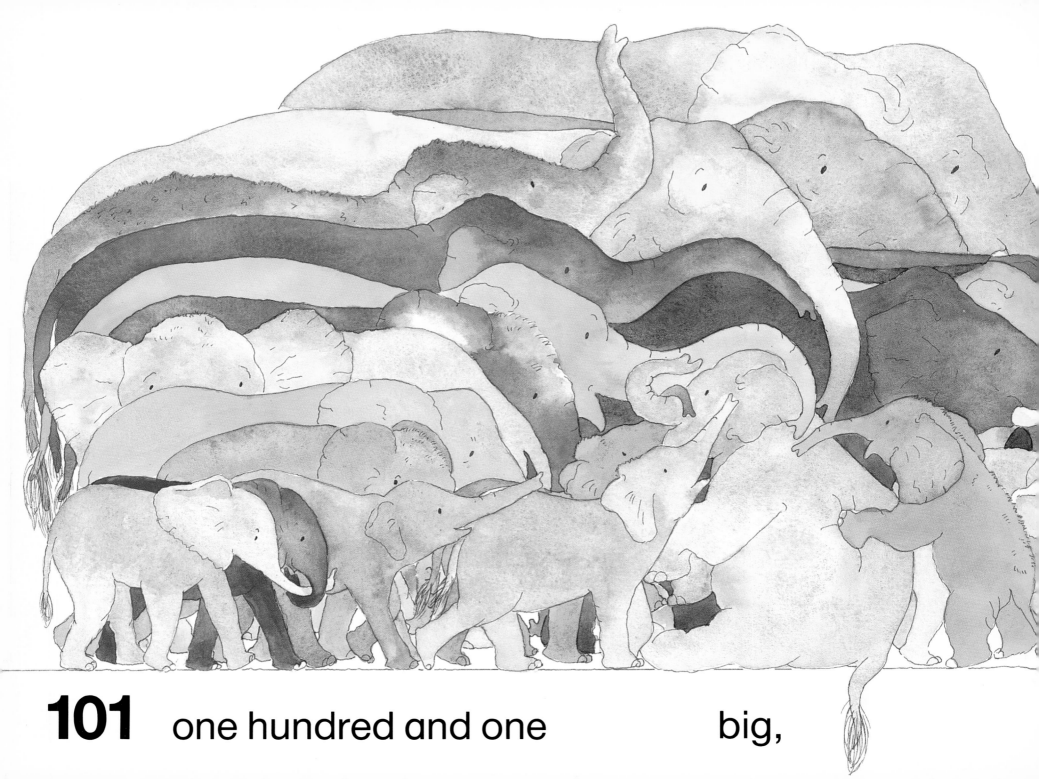

101 one hundred and one   big,

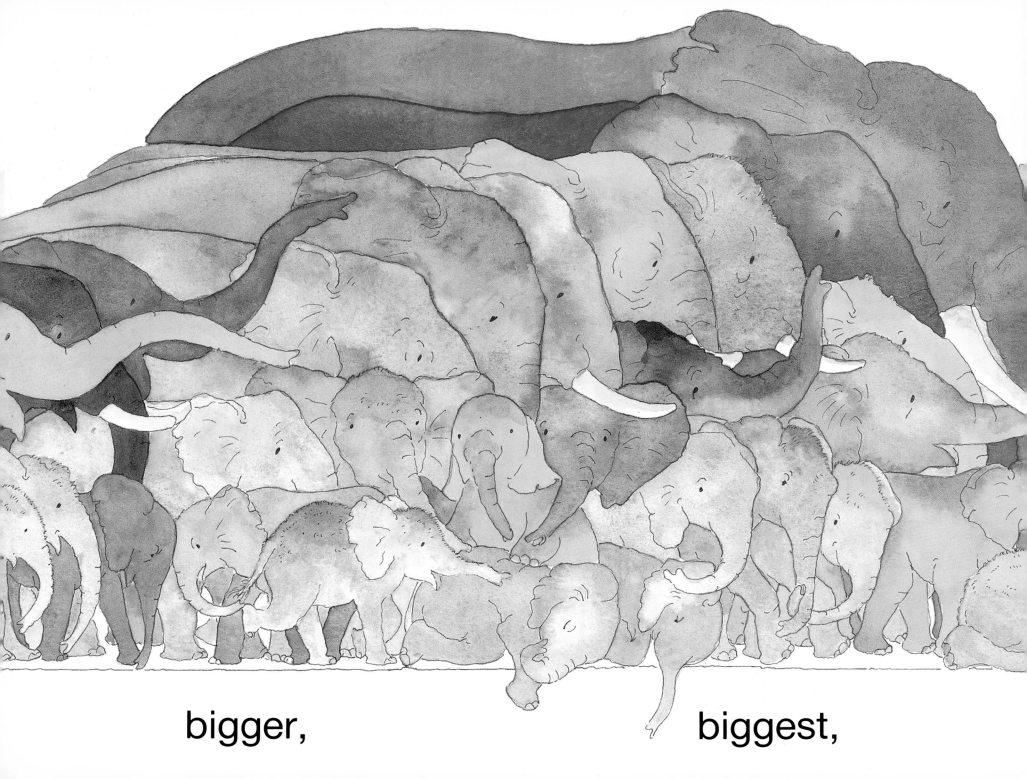

bigger, biggest,

plodding

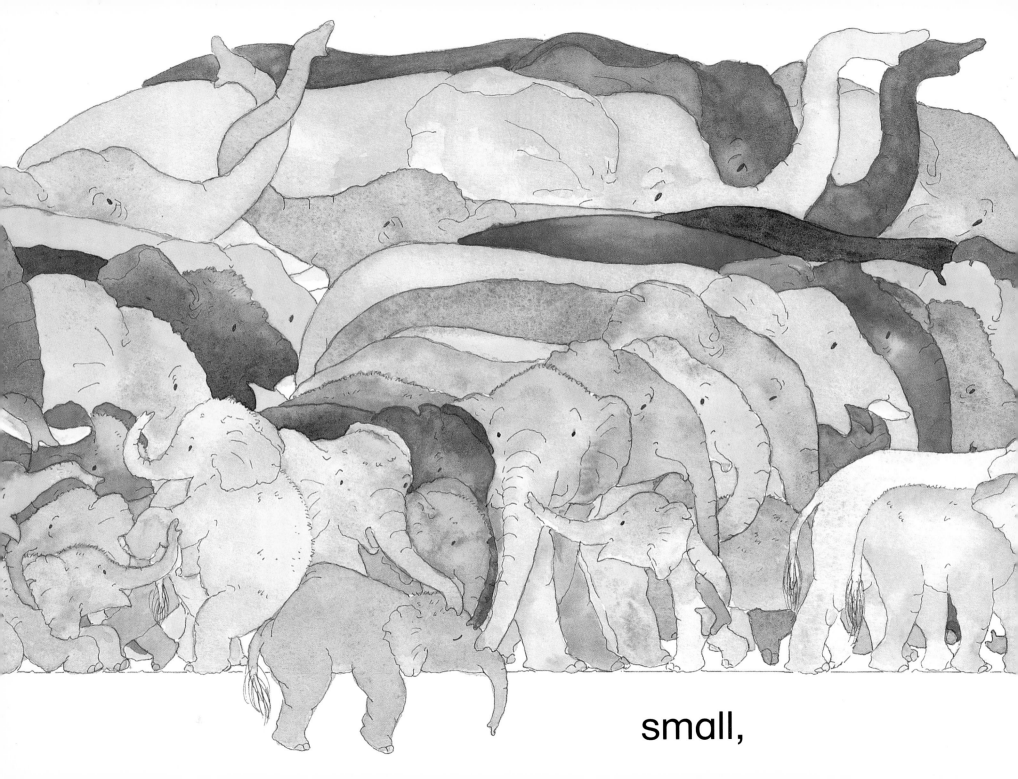

small,

playful,   powerful,